Photo copyright ©Maria Slough

Hello everyone,

At Born Free we believe all animals are individuals,
just like people. Each has its own likes, dislikes, hopes
and fears and all deserve to live their lives without
being afraid of us. Tragically that is not always the
case, but I am hopeful that more and more people

will want to look after and respect the amazing wild creatures who create the world's wild places.

Our story began when my late husband, Bill Travers, and I went to Kenya in 1964. We had been asked to act in a film called 'Born Free' – the first of many books written by Joy Adamson about Elsa, a lioness. Elsa was an orphaned cub whose mother had been shot in self-defence by Joy's husband, game warden George Adamson. Elsa almost became the child they never had, but although she shared their life in the Kenyan bush, the Adamsons were determined she would grow up to be a real wild lioness.

Too often lions are looked on as savage beasts, shot for so-called sport, killed for a trophy. The Adamsons wanted to prove that lions have many characteristics like us – loyalty, friendships, a sense of fun, love of their young. Working on the film and getting to know these amazing animals (none we worked with closely were trained), made a deep impression on us. The seed from which grew the rest of our life.

In 1984, together with our eldest son Will, we founded our charity which, thirty-one years on, continues to strive to end the cruelty, suffering and

Dolphin Rescue

A True Story

Written by
Jinny Johnson

Orion
Children's Books

ORION CHILDREN'S BOOKS

First published in Great Britain in 2015 by Orion Children's Books
This edition published in Great Britain in 2016 by Hodder and Stoughton

1 3 5 7 9 10 8 6 4 2

A CIP catalogue record for this book is available from the British Library.

ISBN 978 1 5101 0132 6

Printed and bound in China

The paper and board used in this book are from
well-managed forestsand other responsible sources.

Orion Children's Books
An imprint of
Hachette Children's Group
Part of Hodder and Stoughton
Carmelite House
50 Victoria Embankment
London EC4Y 0DZ

An Hachette UK Company
www.hachette.co.uk

www.hachettechildrens.co.uk

exploitation endured by wild animals all over the world. And we try to involve local communities to ensure the protection of wild places and the animals who live there.

This story is about two dolphins, Tom and Misha. As you may know dolphins are still caught from the wild ocean, transported to different countries around the world and put into concrete, chlorinated pools where they are taught tricks to entertain audiences who, for some reason, don't seem to realise that these sensitive, highly intelligent creatures are now in a kind of prison. As the people in the audience smile so, they believe, the dolphin smiles too. But the dolphin's 'smile' is the structure of its face. So even sad dolphins can look as if they are happy.

I was very lucky to be there for the last part of this story. All of us at Born Free feel a special joy when, sometimes, our hopes for an animal's future have been fulfilled.

Virginia McKenna

Virginia McKenna
Actress and Founder Trustee, Born Free Foundation

BORN FREE AROUND THE WORLD

Animal Welfare

Born Free exposes animal suffering and fights cruelty.

Wild Animal Rescue

Born Free develops and supports many wild animal rescue centres.

Canada

United Kingdom

USA

South America

Conservation

orn Free protects wild animals
in their natural habitat.

Communities and Education

Born Free works closely
with communities who
live alongside the projects
we support.

rope

frica

China

India

Vietnam

Indonesia

This is a true story about two bottlenose dolphins, Tom and Misha, who were snatched from life in the wild, kept captive in terrible conditions, then rescued by a team led by Born Free. Thanks to months of work by a dedicated team, the two dolphins were eventually released back into the ocean to live free once more.

Tom

FACTFILE

- Born in the Aegean Sea, off the coast of Turkey

- Very playful and mischievous, always getting into trouble

- Likes people – especially fishermen – and this could get him into even more trouble

- Likes to take the easy way out – stealing fish from fishermen is one of his favourite ways of getting food

- Loves to play catch with seaweed and sponges

- Favourite hobby – surfing the waves

FACTFILE

Misha

- Born in the Aegean Sea, off the coast of Turkey

- Quiet, thoughtful and cautious

- Prefers to stay clear of people but likes the company of other dolphins

- Loves his food and enjoys hunting

- Easily sunburned so likes to keep his head out of the sun

- Doesn't like rain

Learn a new dolphin fact every time you see me.

Chapter One

June 2010
Hisaronu, Turkey

'Swim with dolphins! Enjoy the adventure of a lifetime!' Excited holidaymakers gazed at the posters of dolphins leaping in turquoise waters that shimmered in the sunlight as they swam with happy tourists. They couldn't wait for their turn. This would be the highlight of their holiday, a dream come true.

More and more of them joined the queue by the wooden fence on a street in Hisaronu, a mountain resort on the coast of southern Turkey. It was late afternoon, the sun still beat down from a bright, cloudless sky; the perfect time to enjoy a swim with these most magical of creatures.

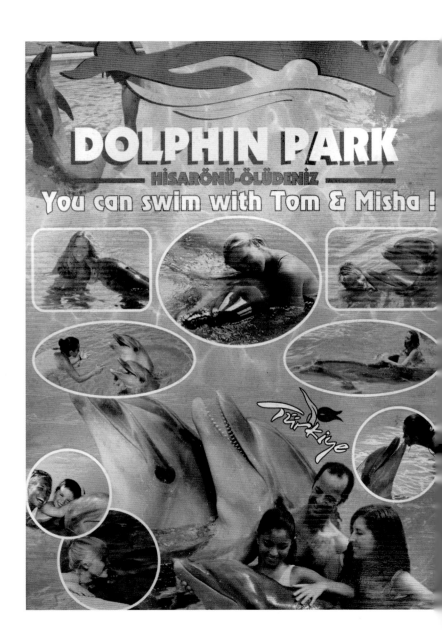

Families paid for their tickets and hurried through the gates, chattering excitedly. But their chatter died to worried whispers as they neared the dolphin pool. Things were not quite what they'd expected. This was not the large expanse of clear blue water they'd seen in the posters. Instead there was what looked like an ordinary hotel swimming pool, except its sides were an untidy mess of broken bricks and crumbling walls. The water was dark and dirty. A smell of rotting fish hung in the air and a few children looked anxiously at their parents and held their noses.

Two dolphins were popping up and down in the water as their trainer hurled fish into their mouths. But they didn't look sleek and glowing like the dolphins in the pictures outside the gate. Their bodies were thin and their eyes dull. When feeding time was over they swam aimlessly away, moving up and down in their cramped little pool. This wasn't what the tourists had been promised, not the experience they had looked forward to for so long.

Gingerly, a few people slid into the pool with the dolphins. The smell of chlorine was so strong it was almost unbearable, and the water felt sticky and greasy.

Music blared from the nearby bars, battling with the call to prayer from the neighbouring mosque. How did the dolphins stand the dirt and the noise? Surely this couldn't be right?

Those people who did venture into the murky water did get the chance to be close to the dolphins. But even though the visitors knew little about a dolphin's life in the wild they could feel that these two weren't happy.

Dolphins are mammals so they belong to the same group of animals as lions, cats, dogs, monkeys – and humans, of course. They spend their whole lives in the sea, but they have to come to the surface regularly to breathe air.

What these tourists didn't know was what had happened to the two dolphins before they arrived at the makeshift pool and just how much they had been through. It's strictly against the law to take dolphins from the wild in Turkey, but these two had probably

Bottlenose dolphins live in warm and tropical seas all over the world. A full-grown dolphin can be more than 3 metres long and weigh more than 500 kilograms –that's at least twice as heavy as a lion and more than 6 or 7 humans. Their body is a streamlined torpedo shape, which helps them move through the water at speed, and dark grey in colour on the back, fading to a lighter grey or white belly. On the dolphin's back is a tall, curved fin called a dorsal fin, and on the underside are two pointed flippers.

been captured in the Aegean Sea in 2006. They would have been between six and ten years old at the time.

It's not easy to catch wild dolphins and it must have been a terrifying experience for them. They were brutally wrenched away from their companions, from freedom and everything they knew and taken to a dolphinarium in Kas, east of Hisaronu on the Turkish coast. From that moment, their lives changed totally.

Wild dolphins are energetic, fun-loving and highly intelligent – perhaps the cleverest animals in the sea.

They love company and they live in groups of anything from two or three to several hundred animals. These two must have missed their group so much, as dolphins are constantly nuzzling and rubbing one another. They touch with their mouths, tap with their fins and even swim close together. Dolphins can be less friendly too, of course. They'll ram with their body or bite and strike with their tail if they're not happy with a companion. Just like humans, dolphins don't always get along and Misha

When young dolphins first leave their mother they may join groups of other youngsters for a while. These young dolphins are active and energetic, chasing and playing to build up their strength. When they are about eight years old the females are ready to mate and have young of their own and they may return to their mother and grandmother's group. Males may continue to move in groups with other males and companions. They stay together for many years forming strong bonds with each other.

sometimes struck out against Tom when he became too mischievous and annoying.

Dolphins make lots of different sounds, including whistles, barks, yelps and strange creaky noises. Like all dolphins, Tom and Misha each had their own special whistling sound. This whistle is like a signature that tells other dolphins who it is – rather in the same way as we tell people our name. A dolphin doesn't make its 'signature whistle' from birth.

It develops the sound over the first months of life and it usually resembles the mother's whistle – just like a young child learns to speak with the same accent as its mother. Dolphins will call out to each other using their whistle and the other animal replies with its own. If a dolphin gets separated from its group or a calf loses sight of its mother, they whistle frantically until they're together again.

Tom and Misha did have each other to talk to, but there was little to gossip about once they were captives. No need to warn each other about approaching boats or sharks. No excitement to share about a big school of fish nearby. Gradually, they grew more and more silent.

Like humans, dolphins play even once they are full grown and enjoy a game together. Tom was especially fun-loving and had probably liked playing underwater catch with a piece of seaweed or riding the waves, just like a surfer! Now his days of freedom and fun were gone. No longer could Tom and Misha swim or frolic with other dolphins in the endless blue ocean waters. No longer could they hunt and catch their own food.

Tom and Misha would have been used to travelling for huge distances, swimming 100 kilometres or more in a day as they explored the expanses of the ocean and searched for food. They would have leaped and somersaulted above the sunlit waves for the sheer joy of it – jumping nearly five metres out of the water, then plunging down. Dolphins are playful, inquisitive creatures, always ready to investigate anything – and anybody – they come across in their ocean world.

Now imprisoned in their concrete pool, they were taught to leap and dive in return for fish and they soon learned that if they didn't do what their trainer wanted they would go hungry. But worse was to come. The Russian businessman who owned the dolphinarium in Kas had decided to expand his business and set up in the holiday town of Hisaronu, two hours from Kas. It was popular with tourists and he thought he might make more money by opening a dolphin park there.

In early June 2010, with little thought for Tom and Misha's health or comfort, he had them hoisted from the pool and taken in the back of a vegetable truck to Hisaronu. It was a rough and ready journey and it's amazing that they survived, with no one to keep them cool and comfortable on the way. They must have been so scared as they were shaken around in the truck for hour after hour.

Once they reached Hisaronu, the dolphins were put in a cramped, hastily built swimming pool in the middle of a noisy nightclub district. The pool measured 17 by 12 metres and was only 4 metres deep, way too small for these large, active animals. Imagine how they must have felt, away from everything they knew and with no one who properly understood how to look after them. Every sound was scary and unfamiliar; every surface hard and strange.

The dolphin's beak is about 8 centimetres long and its mouth curves upwards, giving its face a permanently happy expression. Its jaws are lined with 80 to 100 small cone-shaped teeth.

Tom and Misha's owner was eager to get his money-making business started for the busy summer season and soon opened the gates to his dolphin park. He decided to charge $50 for a ten-minute swim with his captives and at first eager tourists flocked to the pool.

The dolphins had been trained at the previous park and they obediently swam with the admiring visitors. Tom had undergone more training than Misha and was particularly willing to interact with people. Misha did his bit too, for, like Tom, he'd learned that this was the way to get food.

And all the while the dolphins smiled, but their smiles don't show how they really feel – it is just the way their mouth is shaped. How could they be happy, trapped in a pool full of heavily chlorinated water instead of seawater, unable to swim far, unable to be with other dolphins or lead any kind of normal life?

Chapter Two

July 2010
Hisaronu, Turkey

Not only had the pool in Hisaronu been hastily constructed, it hadn't been built properly. The cleaning system was broken and the bottom of the pool was soon strewn with dead, rotting fish. And then there was the dolphin waste. Dolphins eat a lot and poo a lot, and the poo wasn't cleared away regularly. The water became slimy and smelly. The blue canvas canopy that was supposed to shade the pool from the hot sun wasn't big enough and Tom and Misha were getting sunburned. They were spending more time at the water's surface than wild dolphins should and their skin easily overheated.

What's more, Hisaronu was a party town, known for its bars and clubs. The air pulsed with loud music day and night – far from ideal for animals as sound-sensitive as dolphins. Tom and Misha were obviously suffering and the tourists and townspeople became worried about them. Local dolphin lovers formed a group called the Dolphin Angels and vowed to rescue them – and other captive dolphins in Turkey – from their unhappy life.

Together with visitors to the resort, the Dolphin Angels complained to the owner of the park and organised protests, marching up and down outside the site with banners calling for the pool to be closed and for the dolphins to be released. Nearby businesses became concerned about bad publicity and some tour companies agreed not to take people to the pool. Meanwhile, the owner and trainers tried to reassure everyone that the dolphins were fine, that they were happy and well looked after. They were desperate not to lose their trade.

But one look at the dolphins' miserable home told a different story. This was clearly a terrible, stressful life. They weren't getting enough stimulation or exercise.

They weren't even given enough food. Dolphins this size need about nine kilograms of fish a day, but these two were getting only about two kilograms – and that was of poor quality. Tom and Misha, unable to swim far and badly nourished, were getting weaker and weaker. Their faces might appear to smile but their eyes were dark and sad.

The work of the Dolphin Angels (especially Nichola Chapman, Dawne Buyukkoca and Lesley Robinson) and their thousands of Facebook followers attracted more and more attention and support. *The Sun* and other international newspapers picked up the story and the Born Free Foundation in England started receiving lots of complaints through its Travellers' Animal Alert campaign. They recognised that this was a hugely important matter and leapt into action. The first step of Tom and Misha's Back to the Blue rescue had begun.

A Born Free team, including veterinary consultant John Knight, arrived from England and managed to get permission from the dolphins' owner for John to examine Tom. They weren't allowed to see Misha. As soon as they looked at Tom, their worst fears were confirmed.

He was in bad shape and his health was worsening. The vet thought that the animals were still strong enough to cope with a move – but it would have to be soon. If Tom and Misha were left much longer in the filthy pool he believed that they would become ill and die. They were listless and quiet and not calling to each other like they would do in the wild. They seemed to have given up on life, and who could blame them?

Word had spread about the conditions at the dolphin park and fewer and fewer tourists were visiting. Many were concerned not only for the health of the dolphins but also for themselves. No one really liked the idea of plunging into that black, smelly water – even to swim with dolphins. Tests carried out by the Born Free vet

showed that the level of bacteria in the pool was high and there's no doubt it was dangerous to the health of anyone who dared to swim there, as well as for the dolphins. The amount of chlorine was also far greater than it should have been – this can affect an animal's eyes and cause blindness.

The owner's money-spinning idea wasn't working out as he'd hoped. He hadn't paid the builders of the pool and life was getting difficult. When the Born Free team first talked to him he still tried to claim the dolphins were healthy but as the protests grew he closed the pool. Soon, having realised the trouble he was in, the owner left the area and disappeared without a trace. No one ever heard from him again.

Meanwhile the builders of the pool, who were still owed money by the owner of the park, had seized the dolphins, along with diving gear, freezers and so on, as assets. They planned to sell them to get their money back and began negotiations with Born Free. But they wanted tens of thousands of pounds and that was far too much for Born Free to pay – even to rescue Tom and Misha. The team had to say no and return to England, but they didn't give up the fight.

Chapter Three

August/September 2010
Hisaronu – Fethiye, Turkey

In late August Born Free had a call from Turkey. The builders of the pool were threatening to sell Tom and Misha to the highest bidder so they could get the cash they were owed. With the help of lawyer Sule Beder and reporter Donal MacIntyre, Born Free began negotiations once again. It was a tense time and the arguments looked likely to drag on for weeks, until the Born Free expert made a shocking statement. The dolphins would soon die if they were not properly cared for. Everyone realised that if something wasn't done quickly, they'd have no hope of getting any money at all and at last a deal was made. The Born Free team was told they could buy Tom and Misha, but they had to be taken that very weekend or they'd be sold to someone else.

A period of frenzied activity began. Born Free had no time to lose if they were to get the dolphins out of Hisaronu safe and sound. The rescue team, made up of representatives from Born Free, dolphin expert Doug Cartlidge, members of the British Divers Marine Life Rescue (an organisation dedicated to helping marine animals in distress), the Dolphin Angels and others – including a local taxi driver – all worked together to make a plan.

Also involved were members of the Turkish Underwater Research Society (Sualtı Araştırmaları Derneği) and they located a sea pen along the coast,

near Marmaris. It had originally been built for fish farming and wasn't as large as the team would have liked, but would make a good temporary home for Tom and Misha until something bigger could be found. It was certainly a million times better than the pool in Hisaronu.

Moving dolphins is not a simple task. They live their whole lives in water, so are not used to bearing their own weight. Without the support of the water a big dolphin may suffocate, as its lungs can be crushed by its own body weight. And, of course, the water keeps the dolphins cool; without it they can easily get far too hot. The rescuers had no time to build a proper water-filled crate for transporting Tom and Misha so had to do the best they could in the circumstances.

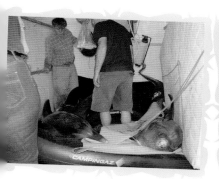

To try to make this difficult journey as comfortable as possible for the dolphins, the team managed to hire a refrigerated truck. At least their precious cargo wouldn't be too hot, despite the scorching summer sun. They begged and borrowed as many mattresses and airbeds as they could find from local people. These were loaded into the truck to provide some cushioning and support for the dolphins during the journey.

At first light on a Sunday morning, nearly four months after Tom and Misha had arrived at Hisaronu, the Back to the Blue team gathered at the pool to start this difficult and dramatic rescue. With the aid of many helpers, the dolphins were lifted from the pool in slings and carefully placed in the truck. It was a tense day for the team but so much worse for

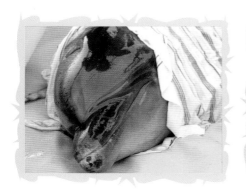

Tom and Misha. Already weak and stressed, they had been taken from the water and put in a very strange and frightening place. They didn't know that this time they were being taken by people who only wanted the best for them. They didn't know that at last they were heading for a much better life.

At least on this journey, every possible effort was made to keep Tom and Misha comfortable. Devoted helpers travelled with them, talking to them and doing their best to soothe their fears. No doubt the dolphins were scared, but hopefully they were calmed by the gentle hands that wrapped them in wet blankets and towels to keep their skin damp and cool.

The journey by road took about four hours but the last part had to be travelled by sea – the road to the stretch of coast nearest the sea pen was too narrow

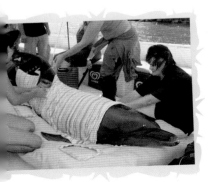

for the truck. The mattresses were piled into the boat and the dolphins were moved yet again. Perhaps at this point in the day the sound of the sea might have raised their spirits and stirred some distant memories of another life. At last Tom and Misha reached the sea pen in a beautiful secluded bay. Yes, they were still

captives – the pen was enclosed by netting to keep them safe, as they were far from ready to live freely again – but life was about to get a whole lot better.

As gently and carefully as they could, the team lifted the stretchers carrying Tom and Misha from the boat into the water. People wept for joy and cheered

as the dolphins slipped into the sea. What bliss it must have been for them after their long journey. How wonderful the ocean must have felt. At first their movements were slow and tentative. They had learned to be wary. But as Tom and Misha felt the cool, clean sea water sweep against their bodies they began to swim. Maybe some instinct told them they were safe once more, back in their natural home.

Tom and Misha had been through so much, but the rescue process was only just beginning. Now they had to learn how to live in the wild again, how to catch their own food and keep themselves safe from predators such as sharks. And no one knew how long this would take.

Chapter Four

October/November 2010
Fethiye, Turkey

Tom and Misha were safe, but all was not well.
They were distressed and quiet. They didn't swim
much and at first they refused to eat anything at all.
As they were already underweight something had to
be done – and fast.

Their Russian trainer, who had worked with them
at the pool, had come along for the first weeks. At
least he was familiar to them among all the strangers
and he was able to force-feed them through a tube.
It was a difficult task, but the team couldn't risk the
dolphins becoming any weaker. Tom and Misha

needed urgent medical attention to treat infections and parasites they'd picked up in their filthy pool. Members of the team were also at risk. As a precaution, the vet, who had spent a lot of time in the pool at Hisaronu, undertook a course of antibiotics.

You might think that since dolphins are so clever they would remember their previous life in the wild and that it would be easy to get them ready for release. Unfortunately not. During the four years they had been in captivity Tom and Misha had become more and more depressed and withdrawn. They had forgotten how to be dolphins. They simply did what was demanded of them – to interact and swim with the visitors.

Dolphins learn a lot of their behaviour from other dolphins. They imitate each other and share information. Tom and Misha had been without this sort of contact and before they could be released they had to learn how to cope for themselves and how to survive in the wild. They had to find out how to live free once more. After the initial excitement of the release the team was worried about how best to care for their charges and how to prepare them for release. Derya Yildirim and Erdem Danyer from the Underwater Research Society (Sualtı Araştırmaları Derneği) were working round the clock, but they urgently needed someone with special knowledge of the care of captive dolphins.

Happily, help was on the way. Born Free contacted Steve McCulloch in the United States. Steve has worked with dolphins for more than thirty years, cares passionately about their welfare and understands how to help them. He agreed to visit

and advise the team on how best to work with the dolphins and bring them back to health. His long experience of working with dolphins told him just what to do and Tom and Misha seemed to realise that here was someone who understood them and their needs. With his great kindness and patience, Steve began to nurse them back to health.

The most urgent task was to get them eating more and putting on weight. Since Tom and Misha had arrived at the sea pen the team had been feeding them more or less on demand, 24 hours a day, but Steve developed a more structured routine and a plan for getting them feeding normally again. For years they had been fed nothing but frozen fish. To them, food was something that came from a trainer's hand, above the water's surface. They no longer knew how

to catch live fish underwater. The dolphins did see fish swimming outside the pen, and many even came into the pen through the mesh, but they didn't try to hunt them. They simply watched with interest as the fish swam around them, rather like we might watch a wildlife programme on TV!

At this point Tom and Misha were being fed eight or nine times a day. Misha appeared to be enjoying his food and ate a little more each week. Tom was more changeable and naughty, sometimes annoying Misha at mealtimes instead of eating his food.

One of the secrets of the bottlenose dolphin's success in the wild is that they are very adaptable: they have many different ways of hunting and they will eat lots of different kinds of fish, as well as squid and shellfish. An adult dolphin may catch up to 15 kilos of fish a day. Groups of dolphins often work together to surround a large shoal of fish, forcing them toward the shore in a tight mass. Members of the group then take it in turns to gobble up the fish, while others stop the rest of the shoal from escaping. Dolphins also sometimes follow fishing boats and snap up unwanted fish thrown overboard by the fishermen. Another feeding method is known as 'fish whacking' – the dolphin slaps a fish hard with its tail, sending it up out of the water and then down into the dolphin's waiting jaws.

As well as learning to catch their own food, Tom and Misha needed to be much stronger and fitter before they could be released. Captive dolphins don't have to move far to get their food – most can't anyway as they are in such a small space. They do have to

leap for the crowds but that's nothing compared to the long distances they might swim in the sea. Wild dolphins are constantly on the move as they travel in search of food, avoid predators such as sharks, and frolic with their companions. Until the team was sure that Tom and Misha could swim fast for many kilometres, there was no way they could be released.

Fortunately, by November 2010 a new larger sea pen was ready for them. This measured 30 metres across and was 15 metres deep, giving Tom and Misha much more room to swim and dive. But first they had to be moved, which was no easy task since they were now much bigger and heavier than they had been at the time of the rescue.

Steve led operations, and the dolphins were lifted out of the water on stretchers, carried on to boats and taken to the new pen for release. Interestingly, Tom and Misha seemed unwilling to be separated, showing that they were fond of each other despite their troubles – and despite occasional squabbles!

Wild dolphins appear to form strong bonds and to help one another. Like many animals they protect their young, but a dolphin may also stand guard with an injured companion to defend it from danger and may also help it to the surface to take a breath. While female dolphins give birth, others stay close to help nudge the newborn to the surface to take its first breath. And dolphins have been known to help humans too. A few years ago some swimmers off the coast of New Zealand suddenly found themselves far too close to a great white shark! A group of dolphins appeared and surrounded the swimmers until the shark gave up and went away and there have been many similar incidents.

FACT FILE

Chapter Five

Steve was able to start Tom and Misha on the road to recovery but he had other commitments and couldn't stay with them for long. In January 2011 another expert on marine mammals arrived – Jeff Foster, who worked with the dolphins and the Born Free team until the animals were ready for release.

For years, Jeff had been involved in capturing whales and dolphins for dolphin parks and aquariums. But then he had begun to question what he was doing and realised how wrong it was to take animals from the wild and use them for human entertainment. He began to take part in the conservation and rehabilitation of marine mammals and has worked in this field ever since. His most high-profile work was with Keiko, the orca featured in the film 'Free Willy'. Jeff did succeed in releasing Keiko into the wild after years in captivity but sadly the orca died the following year. For Jeff, Tom and Misha were a challenge. If the team did manage to rehabilitate

these two dolphins, release them successfully and closely follow their progress in the wild for as long as they could, it would be a first. No one else had thoroughly documented a release. Although some captive dolphins have been set free and sighted afterwards, their activity post-release had never before been monitored so conclusively.

Jeff and Steve knew that Tom and Misha's years of captivity had left them bored and in low spirits. The team had to get the dolphins thinking for themselves again. In the wild there are different challenges every day – changing tides, currents, weather, all sorts of other animals and hazards. A wild dolphin must be constantly on the alert to meet these challenges. Tom and Misha had to learn to use their skills and senses once again and that meant months of dedicated work by the rescue team.

When Tom and Misha first started to eat again at the sea pen they would only take food handed to them by people. They ignored food that was thrown into the water and didn't understand the idea of catching it for themselves. The first stage of retraining was for Tom and Misha to start feeding underwater again. They were still given dead fish but they didn't have to beg for it at the side of a pool.

Tom and Misha were flourishing but they needed to get used to taking live food again. That was to be a long and difficult task. Being faced with a wriggling, living creature would be a real shock if all you could remember eating was lumps of cold stiff food.

And they had to get used to a different diet. When they'd arrived in the sea pen they were fed only mackerel, as they had been in Hisaronu, and refused all other food. The problem was that mackerel are not Mediterranean fish. Tom and Misha needed to learn to eat food such as mullet and anchovies that they would find in the sea once released. Slowly the mackerel were replaced with local fish and eventually they began to accept these.

As they moved around the sea pen more and more their bodies grew stronger and they were becoming dolphins again, whistling and clicking as they competed for food.

Dolphins may not have, or need, a sense of smell but they have good senses of sight, hearing, taste and touch. In order to keep the body streamlined for fast swimming a dolphin does not have external ears, just small ear openings on both sides of the head. Their hearing is more sensitive than that of humans and they can hear lots of things humans can't.

A dolphin's eyesight is excellent too and they can see well both underwater and above the surface. What's more, their eyes can work independently of each other so a dolphin can look down to the dark sea bed with one eye and up to the brighter surface with the other.

But a dolphin's most important skill is echolocation. It works like this: a dolphin gives out high-frequency clicking sounds that pass out through the big rounded part of the head (called the melon). It can make as many as 1000 of these clicks a second. The sounds bounce off any objects, such as fish, in their path. The returning echoes of these sounds tell a dolphin a great deal about the object and help it work out where it is, how big, how fast it is moving and so on – they allow the dolphin to create an incredibly detailed 'picture' of its surroundings. Echolocation helps dolphins find fish hidden in sand on the sea bed and some people say that a dolphin can even stun its prey from a distance by using echolocation

Chapter Six

July–October 2011
Fetiye–Gokova, Turkey

By now Tom and Misha were flourishing and putting on weight. Everyone was working so hard but they were making good progress so their efforts felt worthwhile. Then, about ten months after the rescue, disaster struck. Somehow both dolphins had picked up an infection. They wouldn't eat or respond to their carers and became very unwell. The team was deeply worried. Could all their efforts have been in vain?

In order to receive treatment with antibiotics, Tom and Misha had to be caught and then moved into a smaller 'hospital' sea pen. The team didn't want to frighten Tom and Misha and undo all their good work, so some specialists in dolphin capture were brought in. Their tactic was to lasso each dolphin by the tail and draw it into a sling for transfer to the hospital pen. They had to succeed at their first try, or else the dolphins would get too stressed and be even harder to catch.

Fortunately, the team – now joined by Amy Souster and Mike Partica – managed to capture and transfer Tom and Misha without too much trouble. The picture on pages 66 and 67 shows them in the hospital pen. They were given antibiotic treatment and started to improve within hours. They began to eat and respond again and were soon back to their old selves, ready to move back to the big sea pen. But then there was another setback – trouble with people in

the area near the sea pen who decided they didn't like the dolphins and the team being there. They began to bother the team and caused damage to the sea pen.

Things were getting impossible, when Haluk Karamanoğlu, who owned the Gokova Sailing Club, offered the team a site a little way down the coast. Once again the dolphins were moved, this time in the sea pen, which was hitched to the back of a boat and very slowly pulled to the new location. This was a beautiful secluded bay, where the only sounds were of waves gently lapping at the rocky shores and birds calling in the pine forests fringing the coast; a world away from the noisy streets of Hisaronu.

All the while the team were living on the bay as near as possible to the sea pen, as the animals needed

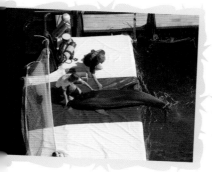

attention 24 hours a day. There were at least four people on permanent duty, joined from time to time by other volunteers. At first the carers lived in a little wooden cottage but later this was damaged by storms and even a tornado, and so they moved into a caravan by the jetty.

It's easy to think that the sun always shone on that beautiful Mediterranean bay but it didn't! Throughout

the winter and into the spring there were days of cold winds and torrential rain, but the work of the rescue team went on. Day and night, in all weathers, the dolphins had to be fed, observed and encouraged to swim and play. Strangely, even though the dolphins lived in water, they didn't seem to like the rain! When there was a downpour they would just poke as little of their noses as possible out of the water.

To overcome the years Tom and Misha had spent in captivity took time – months not weeks – but they were doing well and becoming stronger. Now the team had to get them used to the idea of making an effort to find food. They put fish in a special underwater pipe that Tom and Misha had to play with in order to reach their food. Then they started to use a giant catapult to fire the fish into the sea pen. The fish were dead, but Tom and Misha had to swim and search for them in the water. They were fast becoming dolphins again, whistling and clicking as they competed for food.

Tom had undergone more training than Misha and was always ready to interact with people. He was like a big bouncy dog, wanting to please – but also on the lookout for the easiest way to get food! He was the mischievous one too and treated everything like a game, keen to get attention from his human friends. Misha was more reserved and seemed more thoughtful. Unlike Tom, he never really interacted much with people for fun. His behaviour was more natural and he was alert and constantly checking out his surroundings. He would gaze out to sea from the pen, as if yearning to be back in the wild.

Tom and Misha were together for years so they had to get along with each other. But dolphins are like people – they don't always hit it off just because they are together. Tom was always ready for a game, wanting to play with Misha. He would torment his companion by constantly swimming up to him and shoving him or giving him a nip. Misha would put up with this without complaint for days, then suddenly turn and chase Tom off. Tom would leave Misha alone for a while, but would soon start teasing him again.

FACT FILE

Dolphins are amazingly energetic creatures and they're expert swimmers and divers. When diving, bottlenose dolphins can easily hold their breath for 40 seconds and on occasions can manage to stay under water for as long as 6 minutes.

Wild dolphins are very active. They love to breach – leap above the water – and to slap their tails on to the surface or ride the swell of water made by boats. They cruise along at 6 kilometers an hour, but can speed up to 30 kilometres an hour while chasing prey or escaping from danger.

Chapter Seven

January/February 2012
Gokova, Turkey

FACT FILE

Wild dolphins spend at least half the day on the move, travelling in search of food. The rest of a dolphin's day is taken up with hunting, feeding, being with other dolphins and resting.

A dolphin sleeps in a very different way to us, with only one half of its brain resting at a time, while the other half stays awake and on the alert. A dolphin can't switch off entirely, as it has to stay conscious enough to come to the surface and take a breath regularly.

Once Tom and Misha had got used to finding their food in the water, the next stage was to get them used to eating live fish that had been humanely stunned – so weren't moving. The dolphins were also encouraged to take the fish at different levels in the water. The team began to toss a mixture of live, stunned and dead fish into the water. This meant that not only did Tom and Misha have to move quickly to seize the food, but also they were competing with each other to fill their tummies.

It was important that any association between fish and people was reduced as much as possible, so the team had a variety ways of delivering the food, such as with feeder tubes, slingshots and other devices. When Tom and Misha were doing something the team wanted, such as swimming energetically around the pen, they would launch a fish into the pen with a slingshot. The dolphins would catch it and so came to figure out that the more they swam the more likely they were to catch fish. Now when their carers released fish into the sea pen, the dolphins enthusiastically chased and dived to catch their prey and competed with each other to seize the most food and this improved their fitness.

Once Tom and Misha were eating live fish once more the team had to work on stimulating them, getting them to be more alert. The aim was to keep them surprised and vary the routine to help them meet the challenges they would face in the wild.

Every day they were given different toys to play with – balls and rings to catch, sticks to retrieve. Strange creatures, such as octopus and jellyfish, were put into the pen for Tom and Misha to investigate. Divers swam around them, encouraging them to play. However, they were careful not to get too close. It was important for Tom and Misha not to rely on human company, otherwise they would be more likely to approach humans after their release – and that could lead to trouble.

Learning to catch fish underwater also helped Tom and Misha grow used to spending more time beneath the surface. Captive dolphins spend as much as 80 per cent of the time above the water – that's where everything is happening and what people pay to see. Wild dolphins, on the other hand, spend most of their time below the surface. This shift was a major change needed in Tom and Misha's lives.

The team also had to teach the dolphins to do certain things so they could monitor their health. For example, the team needed to take blood samples from them regularly in order to spot any changes in their condition and to check for any illnesses that could be passed on to wild dolphins in the area once Tom and Misha were released.

FACT FILE

Sharks are the main predators of bottlenose dolphins and many dolphins bear the scars of shark attacks. If threatened by a shark, a dolphin may just try to swim away – fast! If that fails though, the dolphin may turn on the shark and fight back. Stingrays are another danger and dolphins can die if wounded by the sharp poisonous spine on the base of a stingray's tail.

Chapter Eight

May 2012
Gokova, Turkey

Tom and Misha's rescuers were incredibly dedicated to their task. This was an international effort, with people from Britain and the United States as well as from Turkey. For them all, it was a labour of love. There was nothing they wanted more than to see the dolphins swim off into the ocean once more. That was all the reward they needed. And much as they loved the dolphins, as time went on they had to keep their distance – it was vital for Tom and Misha to break the bond with humans and be ready to relate to other wild dolphins. If they tried to bond with humans once released it could be disastrous.

Now the final stage of the Back to the Blue rescue began. The team had to make sure that Tom and Misha were as fit as possible before the great day of their release. They also wanted them to put on extra weight in case it took them a while to start finding food, so they were given extra fish to eat.

Almost two years after Tom and Misha were first rescued from the crumbling pool at Hisaronu, the team decided they were able to cope on their own. They were hunting and eating well, their bodies were sleek and strong and they were full of energy. They were ready to swim through the vast open oceans once more, go where they wanted and catch their own food.

The team had worked for months with the dolphins and knew them so well, but no one could say quite

how they would behave when set free. The thought of letting them go was both wonderful and terrifying. The release had to be timed just right.

The team had decided that spring was best. From then on through the summer there would be plenty of fish in the area – so lots of food – and plenty of other dolphins for Tom and Misha to meet. The weather would be good and although the water would be warm close to the shore, they dolphins would always be able to swim to cooler waters.

First the dolphins were tagged with specially designed satellite tracking devices. These were fixed to the fin on their back so the team could follow their movements for the first weeks and keep a check on their activities for as long as the batteries lasted. In order for the batteries to work for as long as possible

the transmitter was triggered only when the dolphin's fin broke the surface of the water rather than transmitting all the time. The experts believed that if they could track the dolphins for the first few months after their release and confirm that they were doing well, they would continue to thrive.

Then the great moment came. The team gathered with representatives of Born Free from England and the gates to the sea pen were opened. What would happen next? Would Tom and Misha swim straight out, would they leave and come back again? The tension was almost unbearable.

Tom and Misha were cautious at first. They looked out of the pen but weren't sure quite what to think. They'd been captives for so long. Both of them looked nervous and worried – unsure what to do. Finally after about twenty minutes, members of the team tried signalling to Tom and Misha that it was okay to leave the pen. At last, Tom swam out of the gate, then looked back for a moment. Misha joined him and they took off – fast.

Together they sped across the bay, heading for their new lives in the wild. The team watched with tears in their eyes – so thankful that the dolphins were well

and strong but so sad that they would probably never see them again. A film crew in a boat followed Tom and Misha's movements that day and all seemed to be going well. They saw them catching fish with ease and even meeting other dolphins. At last they were able to live as dolphins should.

Life in the wild isn't without problems, of course. As well as the threat of predatory sharks and capture by humans, wild dolphins face many other dangers. Many get tangled up in fishing nets and drown. Dolphins can also be harmed by high levels of chemicals and other kinds of pollution in the ocean, and their lives may be disturbed by boat traffic and marine constructions, such as oil rigs. In the Mediterranean, overfishing can make it hard for dolphins to find enough food.

Chapter Nine

October 2012
Southern coast of Turkey

The team was able to continue following Tom and Misha's movements with the satellite tracking system for a while. For the first week the dolphins stayed together, swimming along the coast. Then, all of a sudden, they went their separate ways. Perhaps Tom teased Misha once too often?

Misha swam off to the Antalya area of the Turkish coast, which was probably where he originally came from. Perhaps he remembered his home range and found his way by echolocation or maybe he used his ability to 'read' the magnetic field of the coastline? No one knows for sure.

Tom, who was always the most interested in humans and the more mischievous of the two dolphins, had other ideas. He started to swim into bays and approach fishermen and divers. People loved to see him, of course, but this wasn't what the team had planned. They wanted Tom to return to life as a wild dolphin and stay clear of humans. If he continued to swim close to fishing boats and divers he was bound to get into trouble sooner or later. And there was a risk that if he kept on getting close to humans he would get captured again.

But Tom was smart and quickly learned ways to get food. He would hang around near hotels where the fish were fed bread by swimmers and so grew fat and easy to catch. He would swim around cruise ships too and follow fishing boats. He started taking fish from the fishermen's nets, picking out the kind he preferred. The fishermen liked Tom and put up with this thievery for quite a while, but eventually the local fishery cooperative contacted the Born Free team. They warned that a large fishery was coming to the area and they would not tolerate such behaviour by a dolphin. If Tom stole fish from them he was likely to be shot. For his own protection Tom had to be caught once more and moved further along the coast.

When the team found Tom, thanks to the satellite tracking, they hardly recognised him. He had gained nearly 70 kilograms and was a big powerful animal. Although surely he must have remembered the humans who had cared for him for so long he didn't like being caught. He struggled and fought at first – not because he was scared but because he was angry!

The team moved him about 1000 kilometres along the coast to the Antalya region, within 30 kilometres of where Misha was at that time, a glorious stretch of coast where pine-covered mountains fringe the deep blue waters. At first the dolphins didn't meet, but when eventually they did they weren't together for long. Tom took off and didn't stop for miles. Perhaps these two dolphins will never meet again.

Tom and Misha's tags only worked as long as the batteries lasted. Now they are on their own and no one knows where they are. Hopefully they are travelling, hunting and playing as bottlenose dolphins should. Maybe they have joined up with other dolphins, which would help them find prey and defend themselves more successfully – dolphins are good at cooperating with one another. Maybe they have even fathered young.

It was a long and difficult task to rescue these two wonderful animals from their terrible life as prisoners in a dirty swimming pool and return them to the wild, and it was the first time such a rescue attempt and release programme has proved successful. Hopefully we are all learning that dolphins should not be kept in captivity to perform for our entertainment. They are magnificent, intelligent animals and they should be left in peace to spend their lives in the sea where they belong.

Tom and Misha were a very special case and not all captive dolphins are so lucky. There are still thousands of dolphins and whales living in zoos and marine parks all over the world. Even the best of these facilities are tiny compared to a marine mammal's home range in the wild and the animals undoubtedly suffer.

In the wild, dolphins live for more than 30 years, some to as old as 50. Captive dolphins, though, may die younger from stress and illnesses caused by poor living conditions. Dolphins are friendly, sociable animals. They usually live in groups containing anything from two or three to hundreds of individuals, but the make-up of these groups may often change.

Wild dolphins mate and give birth at any time of year, although most young are born in spring and summer. The pregnancy lasts about 12 months and the baby is born underwater. When a dolphin is giving birth, a couple of other females usually gather to help her and guide the newborn up to the surface to take its first breath.

Baby dolphins, called calves, drink their mother's milk for 18 months or so but also start to eat fish from about 6 months old. A calf stays with its mother for several years, staying close by her side to learn as much as it can about how to catch food and survive.

These magnificent creatures are sentenced to an unnatural and unhappy life in order to bring a few moments of fun and entertainment to tourists. Helping captive dolphins re-adapt to life in the wild is a long and very expensive task and many of these animals have been locked away for too long for the process to succeed.

Let us hope, though, that Tom and Misha's story will help to make everyone more aware of what it means for a dolphin to be captured and kept prisoner, and stop them from visiting dolphin parks. Let us all be content with a fleeting glimpse of a leaping dolphin in the wild and allow them to live free in the great ocean.

We would like to extend a big thank you to the following people and organisations that made this incredible rescue and release possible. Their resolve and support on this project was truly invaluable and for that we will be forever grateful.

Alan Knight and all at British Divers Marine Life Rescue

Amy Souster

Bill Rudgard/Raw Cut TV

Cem Kirac and all at S.A.D

Underwater Research Society

CNN/Ivan Watson

Daniel Travers

Derya Yildirim

Donal and Ameera MacIntyre

Doug Cartlidge

Dr Ingrid Visser

Erdem Danyer

Haluk Karamanoglu and family at the Gokova Sailing Club

Helen Worth

ITV Good Morning Britain

Jeff Foster

Jim Horton

John Knight

Juli Goldstein

Lauren St John

Michael Partica

Nichola Chapman and the

Dolphin Angels

Steve McCulloch

Sule Beder

Sunday Express

The Sun

Thomson Airways and TUI

Trevor Evans

Wendy Homewood

Woods Hole Oceanographic Institute

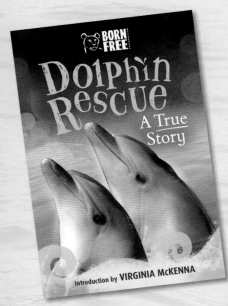

Read all
the rescue
stories

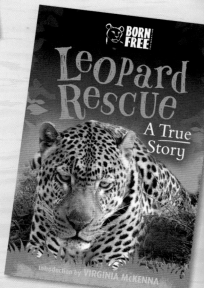

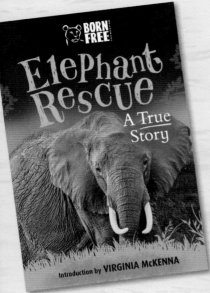

Introduction by VIRGINIA McKENNA

Elephant Rescue
A True Story

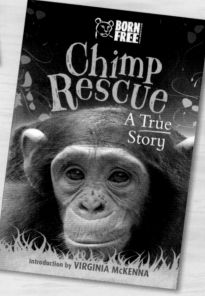

BORN FREE

Chimp Rescue
A True Story

Introduction by VIRGINIA McKENNA

BORN FREE

Lion Rescue
A True Story

Introduction by VIRGINIA McKENNA

BORN FREE FOUNDATION

Go wild with Born Free

Welcome to the Born Free Foundation, where people get into animals and go wild! Our wildlife charity takes action all around the world to save lions, elephants, gorillas, tigers, chimps, dolphins, bears, wolves and lots more.

If you're wild about animals visit
www.bornfree.org.uk
to find out more, join our free kids' club WildcreW or adopt your own animal.

Keep Wildlife in the Wild